INSIDE...

 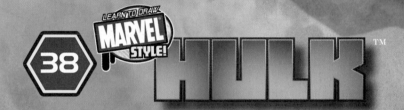
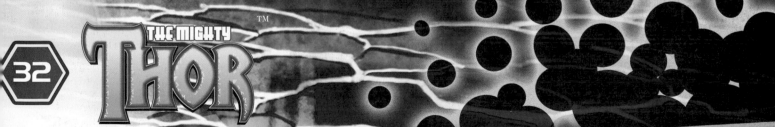

Hey Iron Maniacs! Think you could fly the Iron Man armour? Find out by solving these puzzles!

1 ENEMY ALERT!

MISSION 1

Tony Stark must constantly keep on his guard against a legion of super villains who are determined to destroy him. If you want to wear the Iron Man armour, you'll need to know about of all his nastiest foes!

		I	U	S	P	Y	M	A	S	T	E	R	
I	M	A	N	D	A	R	I	N	K	E	O	C
I	S	T	I	T	A	N	I	U	M	M	A	N	N
O	O	L	C	E	J	R	X	L	W	O	A	D	R
H	G	H	O	S	T	O	S	T	P	O	M	E	B
A	Y	E	R	I	V	I	B	R	O	O	S	N	P
P	O	N	N	S	Y	E	V	O	Y	K	W	W	E
	P	I	R	O	N	M	O	N	G	E	R	S	L
	T	W	S	T	J	J	E	L	I	V	R	

Can you spot all their names in this word grid?

- MANDARIN
- TITANIUM MAN
- GHOST
- SPYMASTER
- UNICORN
- IRON MONGER
- ULTRON
- MODOK
- VIBRO

2 SYSTEM CHECK!

MISSION 2

In the heat of battle, Iron Man often has to reroute vital systems in his armour and perform emergency repairs, all while trying to avoid enemy fire. Test your skills by seeing if you can work out which circuit path will lead to the damaged chip!

A

B

C

D

CHIP

TEST YOUR METAL!

③ ARMOUR EYES!

MISSION 3

Even with its mass of sensors and scanning equipment, you'll still need exceptional observational skills to pilot the Iron Man armour.

See if you've got what it takes by spotting the seven differences between these two pictures!

CAPTAIN AMERICA

STORM

HULK

SPIDER-MAN

GIANT-GIRL

IRON MAN

WOLVERINE

HALT!

Captain America?

LOKI LAUGHS LAST

SUPER-SOLDIER FROM WORLD WAR II. WEATHER GODDESS. SUPER-STRONG ALTER EGO OF SCIENTIST BRUCE BANNER. SPIDER-POWERED WEB-SLINGER. GIANT-SIZED CRIMEFIGHTER. BRILLIANT ARMORED INVENTOR. FERAL MUTANT BRAWLER. TOGETHER THEY ARE THE WORLD'S MIGHTIEST HEROES, BATTLING THE FOES THAT NO SINGLE SUPER HERO COULD WITHSTAND!

Avengers

TONY BEDARD
WRITER

SHANNON GALLANT
PENCILS

NORMAN LEE
INKS

IMPACTO STUDIOS'
ADRIANO LUCAS
COLORS

DAVE SHARPE
LETTERS

CHEN, FLOREA
and GURU eFX
COVER

DAVE SHARPE
PRODUCTION

NATHAN COSBY
ASST. EDITOR

MARK PANICCIA
EDITOR

JOE QUESADA
EDITOR IN CHIEF

DAN BUCKLEY
PUBLISHER

Captain America created by Joe Simon and Jack Kirby

"The *Vault-wagon* was designed to keep the world's toughest bad guys under wraps. *Inhibitor* technology canceled the prisoners' powers.

"But somehow these two knew *exactly* what to do.

"When they destroyed the truck's *generator*, the inhibitors inside it stopped working.

"The *U-Foes* had no trouble busting out once their powers returned."

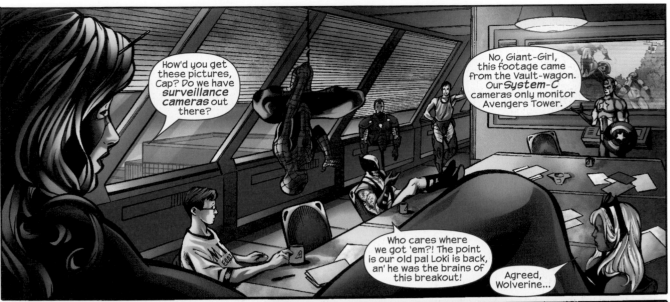

How'd you get these pictures, Cap? Do we have *surveillance* cameras out there?

No, Giant-Girl, this footage came from the Vault-wagon. Our *System-C* cameras only monitor Avengers Tower.

Who cares where we got 'em?! The point is our old pal Loki is back, an' he was the brains of this breakout!

Agreed, Wolverine...

CODE NAME: WRECKER

He also showed up this morning at the trial of *the Wrecker* and helped him escape the courthouse.

Bad enough when we've got to deal with *one* psycho bad guy...

...now they're forming unions.

CODENAME: LOKI
IDENTITY UNKNOWN

"MAGIC" POWERS UNDETERMINED

POSSIBLE ALLIES: WRECKER, U-FOES, JUGGERNAUT

Whatever his motives, Spider-Man, let's *find* Loki before he strikes again!

...and the most *prominent* of these have banded together, calling themselves the *Avengers.*

So I thought, "what if a group of super-villains joined forces to defeat them?"

Works for me. I owe those guys a *greeting* from the land of *beatings!*

Yes, but the *U-Foes* are already a team, and *I'm* in charge...

...so don't go thinking we take orders from *you* now.

My dear Vector, I wish only to grant you *revenge* against the people who put you in jail.

When this is over, you're free to do whatever you wish.

Hey, pal, *all* of us have a beef with the Avengers. If Loki wants to hand 'em to us on a silver platter, why fight it?

Quinjet launch-bay, atop Avengers Tower.

They must have a *hideout* somewhere. We'll start where they freed the U-Foes, and see if they left any clues.

Do we *all* need to go?

If we *find* them, we need to be at *full-strength,* Storm.

Warning! Proximity sensors detect incoming projectile!

We're under attack!

No kiddin', Banner, but by *what?*

Launch-bay doors: activate! Let's have a *look.*

Whoa! My *spider-sense* is tingling like crazy! They must be dropping a hundred-megaton--

--school?!

It's just *floating* towards us...like a cloud...

What if there are *children* inside, and it *stops* floating?

...nhhh...? Whu...m'I...?

Mommy, *look!*

Only in America...

Giant-Girl, *wake up!* I need you *smaller!*

O-okay, Storm! M'shrinkin'...

WHOOOOSOOOOOSSHHH

I feared I'd need a *tornado* to break your fall.

Ow.

I smell like *burnt hair!*

Is everyone okay *upstairs?*

You ladies are *paying* for that hot dog I dropped!

80 stories above...

It would seem my twist on the old "Trojan Horse" trick *worked.*

Now *finish* them! *Humiliate* these pretenders!

The *public* must see that the Avengers are all-too *human!*

The public...?

I'm gonna shake those claws right *off* ya!

Hulk! Gimme a hand!

Your green pal's a little *busy* right now, short-stuff!

KLONGG

HRARRH!

None of you are fit to serve me!

And none of you are *worthy opponents* either!

He's completely *lost it!*

We have to lead him down to the *Meeting Room.* Come on!

No, I think I can counter his--

Oh, *Cap-tain...*

...you disappointed me.

Really, *running away?* Leaving your friends and *this* behind...?

I expected *better* from you, though I'm not sure *why.*

You're not a *god,* after all. You are merely a *man.*

That's always been *enough.* That, and the *country* I stand for.

Nations rise and nations fall. Yours will one day *fade,* as will the ludicrous notion of *super heroes!*

Costumed clowns, craving the same *reverence* that we gods once reserved for ourselves. Bah!

What have we come to when everyone knows a twerp like *Spider-Man,* but precious few remember *Loki, the Trickster?*

So that's the *real* reason you're after us: because you're *jealous.*

For someone who calls himself a "god," that is just *pathetic!*

Perhaps I *am* a bit petty, but that is a secret you will take to your *grave.*

No, Loki. Take a real good look around you. Your secret is *out.*

Eh? What is that contraption?

It's a *camera,* Loki...

...*several* cameras, actually...

We call it *System C.* It's mainly for security.

But it can also send a *live nationwide broadcast,* in case we need to announce an emergency.

What?!

That's right: for the last few minutes, the public you *sneer* at has been *watching* you, Loki...

...they know you're *scared* of people like me...

...and you will never, *ever* win their respect, much less their "reverence."

Go ahead. Turn me into a *toad*, do whatever you want, but it won't change a thing.

We the people know a *bully* when we see one, and we are not impressed.

I should make you *suffer*, Captain. I really, really should...

...but *I*, more than anyone, can appreciate a good *trick*!

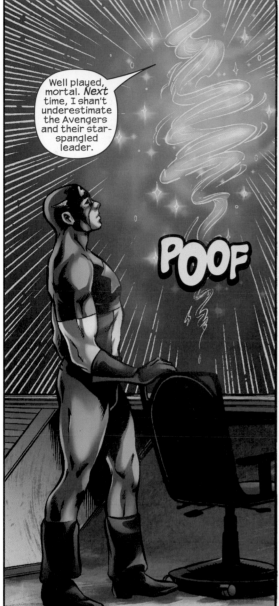

Well played, mortal. *Next* time, I shan't underestimate the Avengers and their star-spangled leader.

POOF

Next time, we'll be ready.

What *happened?* I blacked out for a second, next thing I know, the bad guys are *gone.*

Loki must've *taken* them, but something tells me they'd be better off in jail than with *him* right now.

Not the type to reward *failure,* is he?

Hey, *Cap!* We just saw you downstairs on *TV!*

Did you just humiliate a *deity* in front of three hundred million potential worshippers?

Anyone falls if you know where to hit them.

What was *that* all about?

I'm not sure, honey, but that man's not scared of *anything,* is he?

'Course not, Mommy. He's a *hero!*

The End

LOOK OUT, GUYS AND GALS! EACH OF THE HEROES AND VILLAINS BELOW HAVE BEEN ATTACKED BY AN UNKNOWN ENEMY. USE YOUR PENS AND PENCILS TO GIVE THEM EACH A SPLASH OF COLOUR, THEN DRAW IN WHO YOU THINK THEY'RE FIGHTING!

BATTLE

SABRETOOTH VS. ....

.... **VS. WOLVERINE**

SPIDER-MAN VS. ....

SKETCH!

MAKE YOUR SKETCHES EVEN MORE EXCITITNG BY TRACING OVER THESE SOUND EFFECTS AND STICKING THEM ONTO YOUR PICTURES!

KA-THOOOM

THWIP

SHOOOM

SNIKKT

FWASH

SPAAANG

SHOOOM

KROOOM

VWAAAZZ!

ZZZT ZZZT!

.... VS. STORM

.... VS. DR. STRANGE

LIGHTNING STRIKES TWICE!

Watch out. Marvelites! Thor has just teleported in to warn the Avengers that there are 10 differences between these two pictures! Do you think you can help them out by spotting all the differences?

OPERATION: GAMMA GUARDIAN!

ULTIMATE FIGHTER!

Hulk needs to make sure he uses his most effective moves when battling the alien Champion. Add up the numbers next to each attack to work out which is the strongest.

SUPER PUNCH!

5
+
4
+
2 =

EARTHQUAKE POUND!

3
+
2
+
2 =

GAMMA SLAM!

5
+
3
+
2 =

THUNDER CLAP!

3
+
4
+
2 =

THE STRONGEST ATTACK IS

....

THE MIGHTY THOR

1 POWER PRINCE

Thor is the son of King Odin, ruler of the mystical kingdom of Asgard.

2 BANISHED

Wary of his son's arrogant nature, King Odin forced Thor to live on Earth as a human physician called Donald Blake. Healing the sick taught him a great lesson in humility.

3 HEART OF A HERO

When Odin could see that Thor had learnt his lesson, he allowed him to return to Asgard. But Thor had grown so fond of Earth that he decided to stay and use his god-like powers to help those in need.

4 SUPER HUMAN

All Asgardians are very strong and have much higher levels of toughness than normal humans.

5 OPPONENTS

Thor doesn't just tangle with super villains. Occasionally he has fought beings from other opposing teams such as the super strong Olympian, Hercules.

32

6 TRANSPORTATION
In order to reach Earth, the Asgardians must travel across a rainbow bridge called Bifrost.

7 ROYAL GUARDIAN
The mighty Heimdall guards the rainbow bridge and will only let those pass who have permission of the king.

8 WORTHY
Thor's magical hammer Mjolnir has been enchanted so that only a person worthy of its incredible power can lift it.

9 SUMMON THE STORM
The hammer's greatest ability is its power to summon storms and fire blasts of lightning at Thor's foes.

10 HAND-TO-HAND
Mjolnir has also been enchanted to return to Thor's hand whenever he throws it.

TOP 5...
ALIEN INVADERS!

Hey guys! Space might look peaceful, but there's a whole universe of trouble out there! Get ready for a close encounter as we check out the top five Marvel... *alien invaders!*

5. MOJO!™

Mojo is the ultimate reality TV director! He travels the galaxy capturing super-powered beings and making them fight against each other on his planet, Mojoworld. All of the battles are televised and beamed to hundreds of planets throughout the universe!

He has kidnapped many of Earth's finest warriors in the past, but it was the X-Men who finally managed to defeat him and pull the plug on his insane show!

INVASION RATING:

4. THE SUPER SKRULL!

In retaliation for having their invasion plans thwarted by the Fantastic Four, the Skrull Emperor ordered the creation of the Super Skrull, a being who possessed all of the Fantastic Four's powers! Even though he could stretch his limbs, set his body on fire, become invisible and have a rock-hard skin, Reed Richards defeated him by jamming the Skrull satellite that was beaming him energy, making him as weak as a kitten!

INVASION RATING:

3. THE BROOD!

These insect-like beings, known as the Brood, travel through space looking for new worlds to conquer. They infiltrate planets by laying eggs within members of the native species. When the eggs hatch, the person's body mutates until they are completely transformed into a new Brood warrior! Gross!

INVASION RATING:

2. GLADIATOR!™

Gladiator is the Shi'ar Empire's most powerful warrior. He can fly at hypersonic speeds, lift over 100 tons, fire laser beams from his eyes and is almost invulnerable! Luckily, his big weakness is that his powers are fuelled by his own self-confidence. If you can make him doubt his own abilities, he's guaranteed to go down quick as a flash!

INVASION RATING:

1. SILVER SURFER™

He may be one of the good guys nowadays, but the Silver Surfer used to be the herald of the world destroyer Galactus! Using the mysterious POWER COSMIC to fly through the stars on his shiny surfboard, it was the Silver Surfer's job to find new planets for the giant alien to chow-down on.

Luckily, he realised the error of his ways after visiting Earth and (with a little help from Reed Richards) managed to free himself from Galactus' control.

INVASION RATING:

ARMOUR

GREETINGS, GUYS – TONY STARK HERE. I'M JUST TESTING OUT MY LATEST UPGRADES TO THE IRON MAN ARMOUR AND I COULD DO WITH YOUR HELP. LEND ME A HAND BY SOLVING THESE CHALLENGES!

First up, we need to see how much the new quantum-servos in the arms and legs have improved the suit's strength.

HEAVY METAL!

Find out by adding up the weight of all these things I've been able to lift.

A) TRUCK – 8 TONS

B) LORRY – 10 TONS

C) CAR – 5 TONS

D) ANVIL – 3 TONS

TOTAL WEIGHT LIFTED: ____

TARGET LOCKED!

START →

END

Next, we need to test the new flight controls in a live fire environment. Only problem is that we haven't got all the bugs out of the navigation system yet. Can you help plot a course through this test maze without running into any of the defence droids?

UPGRADE!

O	T	Y	I	B	C	X	A	R	A
M	A	N	D	A	R	I	N	R	L
E	B	S	Q	L	O	V	X	E	Y
Z	A	M	F	P	S	X	D	G	A
N	G	Y	A	Z	S	B	K	N	S
O	H	B	Z	U	B	R	A	O	A
R	O	X	P	K	O	D	O	M	P
A	S	N	Q	N	N	R	V	N	M
B	T	A	J	H	E	G	A	O	X
A	L	Y	M	A	S	B	P	R	A
O	M	A	G	N	E	T	O	I	S

DATA BLAST!

Hmmm... it seems that all the data in the suit's super villain database has been scrambled. Help us get it back in order by spotting all the names hidden in this word grid.

MAGNETO   MANDARIN
MODOK   CROSSBONES
IRON MONGER   GHOST
BARON ZEMO

ARMY OF IRON!

The new suit features a holo-projection unit that can create four hard light copies of the Iron Man armour. See if you can work out which of these is the real thing by spotting which one matches the original blueprint

A.

B.

C.

D.

E.

ORIGINAL:

STEP 1

Firstly, you need to draw the basic shapes that make up his body. Use a pencil to lightly draw the head, shoulders, torso, arms and legs.

STEP 2

Once the basic blocks are drawn, you need to flesh out the body by filling in the arms, hands, legs and feet.

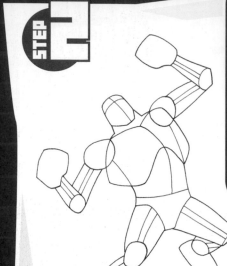

STEP 3

Now you've got the basic shape, start adding details such as his muscles, eyes, nose and hair.

STEP 4

Next add smaller lines to define his muscles and his fingers and toes. Then add the final details like his shorts and teeth.

HULK

Heads up, true believers! Do you think you've got the skills to draw the Incredible Hulk? Just follow these five easy steps and you'll be a *marvel master* in no time!

STEP 5

Finish off by rubbing out your original guide lines and then grab your pens and pencils and get colouring!

TRY IT YOURSELF!

WITH THE GODS AGAINST US

TY TEMPLETON
WRITER

CAFU
PENCILER

TERRY PALLOT
INKER

VAL STAPLES
COLORIST

DAVE SHARPE
LETTERER

GRUMMETT, PALLOT
& SOTO COVER

ANTHONY DIAL
PRODUCTION

NATHAN COSBY
ASSISTANT EDITOR

MARK PANICCIA
EDITOR

JOE QUESADA
EDITOR IN CHIEF

DAN BUCKLEY
PUBLISHER

CAPTAIN AMERICA

STORM

HULK

SPIDER-MAN

GIANT-GIRL

IRON MAN

WOLVERINE

"That covers family members, and much of the *twelve labors.*"

"Finally, we come to a most *popular* legend of *Hercules,* and the reason for the temple below us..."

"According to *myth,* Hercules descended into the *underworld,* and *stole Cerberus,* the giant *three-headed beast* that belonged to *Hades,* lord of that world and *cousin* to Hercules."

SUPER-SOLDIER FROM WORLD WAR II. WEATHER GODDESS. SUPER-STRONG ALTER EGO OF SCIENTIST BRUCE BANNER. SPIDER-POWERED WEB-SLINGER. GIANT-SIZED CRIMEFIGHTER. BRILLIANT ARMORED INVENTOR. FERAL MUTANT BRAWLER. TOGETHER THEY ARE THE WORLD'S MIGHTIEST HEROES, BATTLING THE FOES THAT NO SINGLE SUPER HERO COULD WITHSTAND!

THE AVENGERS

"It led to a feud...a *war...* between these immortal cousins that *supposedly* lasted *centuries.*"

Dr. Bennardo Agro. Head of Archaeological Research, Stark International, Pompei, Italy.

There's a *magnificent* temple dedicated to the legend of *Cerberus* and Hercules, a hundred meters below the ground here.

Buried, like everything *else* in the town of Pompeii, by a severe volcanic eruption of Mount Vesuvius, in the year 79 AD.

Stark International began excavating the temple last week, using the most advanced technological equipment...the most *delicate* of intrusions upon this site...

But, no *sooner* did we commence...

...than the mysterious *earthquakes* began.

Is there a Hercules test later? 'Cause Wolverine wasn't paying attention during the list of wives and kids.

Go stick to a shoe.

Frankly, Greek myths fascinate me. Hercules especially.

Knowledge is power, Wolverine.

I know *one* thing about my powers. Using them to fight earthquakes is a waste of time.

The *Avengers* wouldn't be here if this was a waste of time.

BUS-TED!

You settle down.

After much testing, we determined these earthquakes are *not* coming from Vesuvius, as one might expect.

Instead, the quakes seem to be centered near the temple to Hercules and Cerberus itself...a hundred yards below the surface of the lava rock.

So we took a look underground, using ultrasound radar, which allowed us to see images of the things below the lava rock.

We discovered something very strange.

This is an image of a *huge* carved statue of Cerberus, set in front of the temple below us.

It's *thirty* feet high, and made of solid stone.

What is *more* astounding, is that we've done a dozen Doppler image scans of the ground below us since the quakes began.

And in each of the images, this *three hundred ton* artifact...

...it's moving.

Believe it. This is the start of a bad day.

Not a dog lover, Wolverine?

I don't like messing with the mythological or the immortal, Spider-Man.

A friend of mine used to say, "Ya can't win when the *gods* are against you."

Drop that kind of surrender talk, Avenger.

I'm not surrendering, Cap.

Just talkin' out loud about our chances.

WHACKK!

≶UNGH!≶

Get back, Dr. Banner. You're no good to anyone if you get hurt.

You're right. I'm no good to *anyone!*

Ah.
<That feels better.>

<My lips are free of that accursed crust of rock that stuck to my skin while I was all these centuries entombed. Hercules may speak again.>*

Did he say, "Hercules"?

*translated from ancient Greek. Ye Scholarly Editor.

<You hurl Great Zeus' lightning with such familiarity!>

<Come out of the sky, witch, and speak to me! Are you enemy or friend?>

This is going from bad to worse. Hercules is actively trying to hit me.

If ya can't win when the gods are against you...what are we supposed to do when they crawl out of the ground and make the fight personal?

I told you to stop that "can't win" talk, Wolverine. The Avengers don't quit!

They assemble!

<My sons...>

Hah! <Still remembered two thousand years after their father was trapped in Hades' evil lava flow!!>

I really can't hold it much longer.

Dog must stop hitting Hulk!

And I could use a hand with this monster!

WACK

<Your bravery is like unto my own! To see you stand fast in the face of my righteous rage! Come, let me find you a fine meal.>

What's he saying?

He might be taking us hostage.

⟨Where are you going?!⟩

⟨If you are *truly* Hercules, then you owe us a thirteenth *labor* for the destruction and hurt you've caused!⟩

⟨Who are you to speak to me thusly? I am *indeed* the glorious *son* of Zeus!⟩

Cap's made him mad.

A labor is traditionally what Hercules did to repay the debts he incurred due to anger. In theory--

Please, Doctor Agro, not now.

⟨We need help fighting a giant monster!⟩

Look out! Incoming!!

WHAMMMMMMMM!!

Unbelievable. The Hercules of *legend*. My life's work, breathing and talking to me...

<Thank you for your labor, Hercules. We couldn't have done it without you.>

<'Tis no labor I've just done. I've wrestled Cerberus more times than I can count...>

<And I once held up the entire world to allow Atlas a rest. A mountain is nothing.>

<I still owe you people a great deed.>

<Here. I give this to you...grasp it and summon me when the need is greatest and I shall hear and come to your aid.>

What's he saying?

He says it's a magic ring.

Hold it and call him, and he'll hear it wherever he is.

Seriously?

<I wish I had the time to get to know these magnificent warriors. How like my cousins, the gods, you are!>

<And speaking of my cousins...>

<I have yet to deal with *Hades.* Destroying a city with lava, *just* to entrap me. His destiny is to receive my glorious gift of anger.>

Would any of these grand adventurers care to accompany a god on his quest?>

<We're honored by the invitation, but have duties here on Earth.>

<Farewell, Avengers. We shall meet anon!>

Where's he going in such a hurry?

Family argument. He invited us along...

I choose to remain here... no matter how inviting the offer.

<It was a clever ploy, to raise up the molten ground from the mouth of Vesuvius and encircle me in rock for centuries, Hades.>

<But centuries are the blink of an eye to creatures such as you and me...so I'm coming, cousin!>

<Your wait is at an end!>

ANSWERS

CHIP

C

4 TEST YOUR METAL!

ENEMY ALERT!

ARMOUR EYES!

30

LIGHTNING STRIKES TWICE!

31 ULTIMATE FIGHTER!

$$5 + 4 + 2 = 11$$

**SUPER PUNCH IS TH
STRONGEST ATTACK**

36 HEAVY METAL!
A: 26 TONS

TARGET LOCKED!

START

END

DATA BLAST!

O	T	Y	I	B	C	X	A	R	A
M	A	N	D	A	R	I	N	R	L
E	B	S	Q	L	O	V	X	E	Y
Z	A	M	F	P	S	X	D	G	A
N	G	Y	A	Z	S	B	K	N	S
O	H	B	Z	U	B	R	A	O	P
R	O	X	P	K	O	D	O	M	P
A	S	N	Q	N	N	R	V	N	M
B	T	A	J	H	E	G	A	O	X
A	L	Y	M	A	S	B	P	R	A
O	M	A	G	N	E	T	O	I	S

**ARMY
OF IRON**

**D IS THE
MATCH**